Back from the
DEAD
The Rising of an African Spirit

KNOX MAHLABA

Order this book online at www.trafford.com
or email orders@trafford.com

Most Trafford titles are also available at major online book retailers.

Printed in the United States of America.

ISBN: 978-1-4907-3199-5 (sc)
ISBN: 978-1-4907-3201-5 (hc)
ISBN: 978-1-4907-3200-8 (e)

Library of Congress Control Number: 2014905692

Trafford rev. 03/27/2014

 www.trafford.com
North America & international
toll-free: 1 888 232 4444 (USA & Canada)
fax: 812 355 4082

Curse of ages

Confounding the bearer of news
A messenger without an audience
Like a stream without a delta
Flowing into a tributary
Paying tribute to unknown influences
Studying identified sources
An eye witness to an eye sore
A people torn apart by imaginary differences
Opting to remain silent
Wiping the tears from my eyes
Drying the despair of a people
A curse of ages
A curse placed on a chosen few
The audience ungrateful
Floating like a bottled letter
The message lost at sea
Though the coast is rough
Waiting for the sea to purge itself of foreign debris
Cast the bottle against monstrous rock faces
Shatter the glass ceiling
Toss the message onto the shore
Children dying of hunger
Toy soldiers lying on battle fields
The fields mined with explosives
Mines secured by foreign forces
Our gold lying in Fort Knox
The miners dying
Everybody looking away
Our standing on a downward spiral
Our continent raped whilst we watch
Whilst we pretend not to see, hear no evil!
Though eyes cannot talk
They say so much

Lesson in loyalty

Expensive like a private education
Home schooling away from home
A classroom of bandits
Everybody searching for gold
Panning for substance
Embroiled in substance abuse
The trip very short
The journey too long
Every kilometre away
Every hour a lesson
Learning to be loyal to me
Sharing a desk
Accommodating others
Ignoring personal circumstances
Loyal to the common purpose
Purposefully using each other for personal gain
Portraying loyalty
Duty bound by a pact
Between us
Me, myself and I
Between heart and mind
Body and soul heavenly property
Being there for someone else
Me someone else
Held together at the seams by a notion
Pretence will do
State property, save for loyalty
A sense of belonging so crucial
More important than the air we breathe
Held together by belonging
My loyalties lying somewhere else
Belonging anywhere but here

My Property

Falling on my sword
My property
Embracing reality
So pragmatic
So hectic
Like falling on a sword
Failing to believe
Losing belief
Even faith in your only truly possession
My property a liability
Eating away at my assets
Like a pandemic
An academic subject
Looking back unpredictable
Research a different perspective
Everything laid bare
Exposed so thoroughly
Beached like a whale
Stab wound after stab wound
Dressed in a thick skin
Bearing old scars
My property
Nature's indulgence
Falling on a sword
So foreign
Assegai's stab the enemy
Swords kill important ways
Standing away from a fight foreign
So crucial
Principles are like swords
Trying to hold onto my assegai

Kilimanjaro

A snow-capped mountain on the Equator
Standing apart, standing alone
Africa's greatest mountain
Created by quiet rumblings from beneath
The Rift Valley scarring the surface
Shaping the landscape
The fractures below invisible
The divisions above clear
A people divided
Apportioned by foreign forces
The people apportioning blame
Having a mountain to climb
Very few reach the apex
A few die trying
Having a purpose
Arriving at the summit
Africa's greatest mountain to climb
Standing next to each other too often
Never standing together
Pockets of myopia found all over the place
None standing apart
Stand on principle together
Deep markings of dissatisfaction painted with blood
The way down pulling us down
Too many standing below the summit
Too afraid to meet a challenge
Climb Kilimanjaro
It's our mountain after all
Continental plates cracking below
Splitting apart above
Resembling a shattered windscreen
The pieces mighty together

Futile apart
The climb treacherous
Having my own mountain to climb
Gathering my thoughts
Becoming together
Collecting myself
Connecting myself
The people remember
The apex beside the point
Doing it together the point
Pulling each other upwards
Collect ourselves
Gather ourselves
Remember who we are
Kilimanjaro standing witness
A mountain of greatness
Giving life a purpose
Remember Africa!

Bottled Letter

When a bottled letter washes onto your shore
Your eyes light up
Curiosity invites you to remove the cork
Anticipating the contents
Wondering about the recipient
Empathising with the author
A sailor in distress
Sending out an SOS for his soul
Reading a message not intended for you
Like perusing a diary of the dearly departed
A reading of a last will and testament
Though shameful and intrusive
It's only natural
Envy compels you to break protocol
Yet you'll never open a sealed envelope
Will I ever receive such a letter
An affirmation of compassion
A cry for me
I too would love to drink from this well
Though we conquer the oceans seeking treasure
None can compare to love
Watching the waves come and go
Watching sailors embrace their loved ones for one last time
Waiting for my bottled letter
Dying to quench my thirst
Drink from Cupid's spring
There's nothing better than love
A duet from beyond the grave
Luther and Gregory were so right
Kings have abdicated thrones for a sip of love
Some have gone to war
To secure their heart's desire

I too would throw away a crown
An empire for that matter
A foolish thought I know
Yet there's nothing better than love
Nothing you say, can sway me
Yearning for the other half of my heart
The last piece of a puzzle
A life lived without an attempt to fill your heart's content
No matter how futile the attempt
Is a wasted life
Double or nothing I say
JFK's eternal flame still burns
In Jackie's heart!

I am a Khafre

I've been called by many a name
Childhood nicknames
Family pet names
Apparently what I call myself immaterial
Others choosing to christen me as they choose

Forced to carry a foreign name
A name alien to my culture
Bear the load of an unwanted name
Given many such names
Some do not appear in any documentation
Aliases used behind my back
Boy, Nigger, Thug

Inspired by The Champ
Like Kunta Kente
Forsaking his slave name
Opting for a chosen identity
Embracing his heritage
Ali the Great
King of the Rumble in the Jungle

Chanting Ali, Ali, Ali
Turning my back on Confirmation
My apologies to The Pope
The Vatican can do without another convert
I don't want another unwanted name

Aiding and abetting Kwame Ture
Killing Stokely Carmichael
Lynching Cassius Clay
Burying Dona Richards
Forsaking all my unwanted names

Deemed a kaffir,
aka kafir
Forgive me
For raising such a thorny subject

It's been piercing my heart for years
My people insulted, denigrated
Being black 'n beautiful
Their only crime
Subtle connotations
Houseboy, Sambo, natives,
Harsh expletives, obscenities, cuss words
Negro, kaffer
Unknowingly anointing me

Biko said I was Black
Sobukwe called me an African
Mbeki broke it down for me
Rasta calls me King

Inspired by others too
John Carlos, Tommie Smith
In the summer of '68
Taking gold and silver
Making an important statement
Reminding us
Individual glory doesn't supersede the struggle

Surprised by others like me
How they embrace their unwanted names
Embracing my unwanted name
For I do not believe in foreign notions
God was always here
There's no need to mail order His presence

No longer disputing their claim
For I am an unbeliever in their eyes
In their version of history
In their concoction of religion

Witnessing the birth of Africa within me
Listening to the marimba drums beating from within

I am a descendent of Khafre
Son of Khufu
The fourth King of the Fourth Dynasty
The Great King of Egypt
Commissioner of Pyramids

Yet all they see is just another kaffir
They say the pyramids were built by aliens
Yet all the statues look like Michael Jackson
Their noses falling off
Broken off
To conceal evidence of their blackness
Their likeness to me

Renaming myself
Retaining my naming rights
Reclaiming my identity

Embracing who I am
Who I choose to be

Decorating their paper gold with images from Kemet
Destroying libraries of African documentation
Under the guise of an Arab Spring

Maybe I am an alien
'Cos I resemble the people who built the pyramids

I do not entertain what they say about us
Let alone what they will say about me

My lineage is Khoi and San
Dashed with Bantu soul

I am an African
A son of the soil

Creator of my dynasty
Architect of my legacy
I am a Khafre!

Groove Dynamics

Erupting with feeling
Feelings from where
Yesterday's mudslide
An avalanche so overwhelming
The lava flowing
Burning a soul
Fortifying the core
The earth a womb
From where that is the problem
Earthly feelings basking
Calming torrents
Waves of confusion
Born with a birthmark
A heavenly choice
Choosing a certain way
Chosen by whom
So much like the earth
A dark shade of earth
Watching my own birth
Falling down a black hole
The surroundings a reflection
Making my mark
Brick by brick
Marking a making
Doing what the earth wants
Under duress!
Listening to the force of nature

The Spotlight

When the time comes
Events fall into place
Scenes colouring an image
Dreams just yesterday
And the day before
The world choosing to meet you halfway
'Cos no matter how vivid
Images out do dreams
Different from reality too
When the time arrives
Images match reality
Every moment seamless
Feeling bigger than I am
Larger than star
A damn constellation
When the time arrives
Dreams come true
Flowers blossom in winter
Robins sing soprano
The rain drizzles softly
Whilst the sun bares all
Leaving me to bask in the spotlight
Polishing my shade of black
Hogging the spotlight
When the time arrives
Faith stays
Doubt departs
Staying true to myself

Caught Forever

(A tribute to Nelson Mandela)

Escaping tradition
Running away from responsibility
Only to be caught
By a greater responsibility
Chiselled by a quarry
Bathed in salty water
Seasoned by kelp
Banished to an island
Never forgetting
No man is an island
Even royalty
Heeding a calling
Caught forever
The trap Sisulu's making
Tightened by Tambo
The nation falling onto the safety net
Thank you *Tata*
For clenching your fist
Hoisting it in defiance
Shouting at the top of your voice
"Amandla!"
Thank you Madiba
For taking your gloves off
Raising your hand
Volunteer #1
And taking up arms
Against domination in whatever form
Fighting for freedom of the individual
Defeating fear

Reconciling opposing poles
Only a boxer
Could outflank the status quo
Sip tea with a pariah
Lift the Webb Ellis trophy
Scoring a goal for the people of the south
You're a striker
Umkhonto We Sizwe
Dankie san'!
Siyabonga!

Wedding Vows

Am tired of playing
No more games for me
Tired of cheap thrills
One night stands
Stolen kisses
Unscheduled meetings in the boardroom
I am discarding old flames
Starting anew
Am naughty by nature
Yet I am tired of getting up to no good
With everybody but you
No more OPP for me
You my dear are my canvas
I want to paint a picture of love
Take off your garments and pose for me
Stuff the neighbours
The nay Sayers
We gonna rumble
Do all the wrong things for the right reasons together
Quickies in the back stairway
Smuggle you into the john at the club
Drive you up the wall in an alley
Get to know your geography from north to south
Get lost in your Bermuda Triangle
Lose my tongue in your bush
Plant you behind the trees in the park
And watch blossom into the woman I have always desired
No more cheap thrills for me
I want cosy up to you by the fireplace
Watch my black book go up in flames
I want my own pie
Home baked!

Put my finger in it
Taste your homemaking skills
Make love to you in the hallway
By the entrance hall, in the pantry
It's our house by the way
Stuff the kids
How the hell did they get here?
Watch you walk in the mall
Fully aware you got nothing on underneath
Yearning to get home
Dying to get some
Ditch the kids
Turn on the charm like I just met you
Turn off the lights
Cook a candle lit dinner
Candles in the bathroom
Shower you with love
Disrobe you
Put on some old school
Let Teddy Pendergrass do what he does best
Play games with you
Rekindle our flame
Do my matrimonial duties with a smile
Watch you play with your toy
Keep me interested honey
I'll keep my wedding vows
Like I promised

Piece of the past

Still photographs of rural settings
Black and white in British camps on foreign soil
Housing our own on Robben Island
Isolated from the mainland
Living without heritage

Staying in squatter camps
Informal settlements meant to dehumanise the population
No different from matchboxes
Worse in every respect
Free houses on the market
Inhabitants cheated of ownership
Citizens of no man's land
Living without heritage

The past reincarnating in the present
Correctional facilities packed
Too many people living behind barricades of security gates
The majority far from secure
Society devoid of leadership
'Cos homes are manned
Built with a cultural reference point
A piece of the past

Staying true to chosen virtues
People defining tendencies
Shaping a way of life
Too many houses
Too few homes
Villages of family

Displaced by bachelor flats
Harems of pleasure
Disturbing images of urban settings
Capitalist concentration camps
Destroying a way of life

Local content homeless
Straying from a path
Sense of direction lost
Needing a piece of the past
A revolution

Homes with parents
People with a legacy
A dying population
Living without heritage

Export Quality

Coconuts in free fall
The birds and the bees in flight
Butterflies adding colour
To an already colourful backdrop
The first fruits ripe
Devouring turgid melons
Enjoying a watermelon on the veranda
Licking juices off lips
Taste buds on a tropical retreat
Surrounded by juicy fruit
Full bodied grapes
Perky pears
Exotic dates
Forbidden fruit
Adam's predicament not going away
Lost in an orchard
Struggling to enjoy in moderation
Supermodel peaches
Leaving the best for last
Tasting natural born goodness
Fruits draped in fertility
Picking fruit with care
Export quality only
Making a fruit salad
Contrasting tastes complementing each other
Black berries divine
The harvest coming

My Fault

Interrogating myself
My people
My gender

Looking at me
Mystified by our history
Searching for a stolen legacy

Embarrassed by males
People like myself
Failing to become men
Lacking leadership

The black family in disarray
Family reunions a thing of the past
The black man absent without leave
Fighting other people's wars

Working far away from home
Far from his frame of mind
Locked up in Attica
Absentminded in his home
Detached from his soul
His soul mate seeking solace from elsewhere

My fault

His queen a shadow of her beautiful self
Blemishing the work of the Creator
Mutilated like The Sphinx
No longer the lioness we knew

A castle without a king
Defeats the purpose of the exercise
Let alone a queen without her king

A bold black warrior
A father to her offspring
A shoulder of strength
Rockin' my locks

My crown

Too timid to try tackle the trouble
Too afraid to fight on my own

My ancestors my strength
My children my responsibility

My heart my spear
My history my shield
My heritage my spirit

My Africa my home
My Diaspora my family

My wife my sister
My daughter my mother

My Diaspora my people
My brothers my sisters

Africa's Renaissance, her revival

My purpose

Definition

Blank like copy paper
Cutting careless fingers
Lying in the tray
Awaiting an interaction with ink
Instructions from management
What lies ahead nobody knows
Minutes of a meeting
An envelope maybe
The crush before the trash bin
Dreaming about the comforts of a frame
Guaranteed nothing
Possibly the ink is finished
Tired of being blank
Having no clue whatsoever
Perpetually lying in wait
Any scribble will do
Tired of the same
Wanting definition
Playroom paint brushes
An inspired imagination
Anything to bring colour
Too bland at the moment
The forest too far for a return to the wild
The eventuality closer
A final destination
Printed with words
A picture of something
Anything but this
Even the wings of an aeroplane will do
Instructions from above
A defining moment

Wonder Woman

Burdened by responsibility
The world on her shoulders
Carrying the future in her belly
Caring for the young
Entertaining a fulfilling a career path
A part-time professional
A full-time care giver
A tumultuous balancing act
Like carrying pails of water
Establishing a platform for courtship
Quenching a thirst for love
Blessed with buckets of magic
More than a chick
Ruling the roost
Reigning supreme over hearts of men
What would the world be without her
World war after world war
Women the bedrock of society
The bride the star of the show
The groom only an accessory
Befitting of weddings
Choreographing birth and death
Without her a man's funeral is incomplete
Life impossible
Her presence priceless
Bringing sanity to the institutionalised
Her healing power felt in wards and hearts
Fortifying her man with dignity
Without her, man is nothing
Each day in her company a spring day
Women the bedrock of society
Imagine the world without Palesa no-Mbali
Too ugly to contemplate

(*Palesa - SeSotho word for flower; Mbali - IsiZulu
word for flower; both are names for girls)

Back from the dead

Coming back from the dead
Rising from the ashes
The Earth rumbling from within
From within the hearts of a few good men
Sons of mummies
Soldiers of reason

The truth awakening the dead
A continent staking its claim
Reclaiming its legacy
Its history disputed
By those with no history
With no story of their own

Filing a paternity suit
Africa wants her sons and daughters back
Fighting for custody of their minds
Please appease Nas
Free her sons from corporate prisons
And send them back to Africa
Where they can roam free
Experience a homecoming

Africa is born from within
According to the Gospel of Marimba Ani
The Diaspora extended family
A nomadic family
Africa awaits an embrace
A family reunion
A homecoming of mind sets

Paging papyrus
Reading the Book of The Dead
Disciples born everyday
Revealing a wealth of knowledge
Exposing fairy tales
Seeking conscious minds to spread the word
Emcees to break it down
Tell the people the truth
Plant reeds of thought
Toil the soil
Freedom will flourish on fertile ground
And overflow like the Nile

Coming back from the dead
Rising from the ashes
The earth rumbling from within
From within the hearts of a few good men
Sons of mummies
Soldiers of reason

Veterans of a cultural war
Retracing their steps
Finding the truth
Civilization upon civilization
Circumstantial evidence
The writing on the wall
Evidence of a glorious past
Instructions to a greater future

Africa speaking up
The truth is compelling
Carving warriors out of cowards
Deemed an impossibility by some
Yet an African sits in the Oval Office
A sign of things to come
Standing atop Kilmanjaro
Like Martin we may never see the Promised Land
Like many before who planted seeds of freedom
When the African Spring arrives
The world will be a better place
No more hungry mouths
Every person having value

Hurdling over graves
Taking the baton
From champions of our struggle
Hounds or no hounds
We'll make a run for it
We'll reconstruct the Underground Railroad
'Cos nothing can stop a determined people
Let alone a congregation of souls

A united spirit
Surviving the Middle Passage
Preserving its life
Paying dearly
A whole-lot-of-cost

Cryptic Puzzle

The world a cryptic puzzle
Society's underbelly filled with pacts of secrecy
Trysts of passion between secret lovers
Hidden intentions and traits
Hidden files and folders
Classified material seeping beyond bureaucratic bungles
Truth leaks into a pool of gossip
Rumours picked up randomly by ears and eyes
A dubious methodology
Arriving at the truth by accident
Struggling to stay afloat in a dam of conspiracy theories
The world providing clues
Crafting situations that reveal your true self
Pitting creation against evolution
Forgetting that nature nurtures nurture
The truth like water
Filtering through cracks in a rock formations
Gushing out into the open
Destroying dynasties and commoners alike
A choreographed outburst giving birth to scandal
Yet nothing surprises in a universe of possibility
Especially where intellect lies
Circumstantial evidence an eye witness
Identifying the killer by finding the motive
Though colourless like water
Truth is tainted by spiritual understanding
Subjective in its purest form
Data far from factual minus context
At best an interpretation of perspective
Finding truth a journey with no end
A disappointing destination
Arriving posthumously

Schooling Us

(A tribute to Martin Luther King Jr.)

Decrying inequality
Preferring a peaceful path
Walking to Selma
Marching to D.C.
Writing a letter for the struggle for freedom

Standing your ground
Standing tall
Remaining upright
Taking the high ground
Placing your family at a peril
Preaching from the pulpit

Speaking from the bottom of your heart
Schooling the world in public speaking
Delivering a powerful message
I have a dream…..

Giving us a chance
Acknowledging freedom comes at a price
Taking the bullet for us

Ultimately

Everything going full circle
The seasons too
A cycle of natural causes
Everybody experiencing each season
At a different time
In no particular order
Depending on your concept of God
Your global positioning
The alignment of the stars
The complexion of your character
Your income bracket only a buffer
Cos life has a sense of humour
Frugal with joy
Generous with uncertainty
Yet when the celebrations arrive
We tend to forget
Everything goes full circle
Experiencing fall in winter
Celebrating the rainbow after the storm
Your choices a figment of your imagination
Ultimately!
Your concept of God having the final say
Forcing me to write against my will
Compelling you to read
Appreciating the storm that gave birth to the rainbow
Looking at the silver lining beyond the clouds
Embracing fate!

Wanting a bouquet

A spectrum of colour
In full bloom
Perpetuating nature's arrogance
A picturesque setting
Ruffled by a slight breeze
Shades of beauty

Chocolate, Café Au Lait, Coffee
Lying in the eye of the beholder
All flowers are beautiful
Black is beautiful
Words spoken by Negroid lips
The thoughts of a liberated mind
Witnessed by the naked eye

Epitomised by almost bare maidens
Adorned with something softer than silk
Nubian skin tones
Tall miss things
Figures of speech

Carrying the necessary baggage
Dark skinned honeys amazingly beautiful
Beauty shaped by more than nature's indulgence
It's all in the attitude
Mounds and mounds of it

Bringing colour to an otherwise bland existence
Heads crowned with the artistry of agile fingers
Always shoulders above the rest
Armed with a tantalising laugh
The full stop an equally beautiful smile

Accentuating the richness of full bodied lips
A songstress in stride
The choreography of her movement
A melody to the eyes
The proportions exact
The possibilities amazingly possible
Left only to appreciate the floral arrangement

Wanting a bouquet
Gazing at a picnic spot
Surrounded by pastels and petals
Evoking memories of spring
A different kind of season
Butterflies competing with flora
A contestation for attention
A spectrum of colour

Basking in the laughter of summer
The memory of a smile melting this winter
Confronting nature's contradiction
Though all flowers are beautiful
Only one can be magnificent at any given time
This moment belongs to you

Celebrating Freedom

Standing on the banks
Watching memories of Blood River
Visiting my Waterloo
The water negotiating a difficult path
Meandering the peaks and valleys of a past
Naivety compromising a future
Recalling each defeat
Celebrating every victory
The singing of uniformed school children in the streets
Music to my ears
Interrupted by gun shots
Remembering every bullet I evaded
Living the one that hit
Comprehending the disappointment of bulls eye
Ouch!
Pleading with the heart
Attempting to manage the haemorrhaging
The thorns of childhood
Colluding with voodoo needles
Cursed by misjudgements
Errors of empathy
Good intentions misleading
Evil intent a more reliable source
Delivering what you deserve
As opposed to the opposite
Treated like a slave
Remembering every drop of blood
Each drop shed
Yearning for air
Wanting to breathe
Freedom a costly preoccupation
Using the past to shepherd the future

Hammock

I want to live there
An island in a sea of logic
Suspend myself between palm trees
Where reason is unnecessary
A serene environment
Where the heart governs

Everything simple
Waves going about their business
The sky as alluring as ever
Where my soul can soar
Like the migrating birds
No grammar, no rules
No flight plans
So the heart can be as foolish as it wishes
Right 'n wrong a figment of the imagination
Where the subconscious resides
An open plan with a view

The air filled with chirps and tweets
The space between reason and fear
A figment of my imagination
Where errors are encouraged
Corrections frowned upon

Suspended between fantasy and reality
My field of dreams
My station in life
Where the spirit lies
The subconscious a beautiful place

Departures

Letting go
So often spoken about
So easily
Letting go of what's gone
So difficult
Tearing a part of you away
So easily
Dumb stricken by a loss
Everything gone
Abstract and tangible
Bits and pieces close to the heart
A totem pole here and there
A far memory of a moment
Anticipating loss
So difficult
Spiritual terrain so open
Ancestors in a trance
Omnipotence serving humble pie
Losing appetite for sweet and sour
Spoken sentiment a separate entity
So different from felt sentiment
Open heart surgery
Only without anaesthesia
Yesterday gone
Tomorrow boarding now
So often off-schedule
Here at this very moment
The task at hand
Letting go
So liberating

Pebbles

Tossing pebbles into the river
Disturbing the peace of my surroundings
Taking things easy
Seduced by the anti-establishment lobby
Resigning from the rat race
The establishment has never done me any good
Trotting from totem pole to the next
Taking note of the sweet scents of the forest
The smell of danger in a jungle
Suffocating in the fumes of its urban counterpart
Taking in all the shades of green and its neighbours
Allowing life a voice
Dancing to its melody
Prancing into step
Kicking stones out of my path
Hoping to savour it all
Aware that a saviour may be required
Accommodating sorrow
Celebrating life
Satisfying my soul
The path to an orgasm
…is the orgasm
Aaaah!

Extravaganza

Love meaningless
Only a wrapping for lust
An ad in the singles pages
The need for company a compromising condition
A task embedded in the genes
Lying to each other
Writing poetry with the heart
Flattering another soul
Loins doing the thinking
Acting out a fantasy
Love a theatre of the soul
All the genres included
Drama, tragedy, musical
Love a romantic comedy
A sketch of a predicament
Feeding the appetite of an insatiable audience
Lying to ourselves
Love a reconnaissance mission
Fashioned by the destination
Coming to a heavenly gasp
The physics of attraction harbour no sentiment
Wrapped with trappings
Kisses and hugs
Thoughts of forever
A semblance of innocence
Making love meaningless without the trappings
The spark a handsome ribbon
Tying the contents together
Bodies are only playhouses
Biology an extravaganza

Cried within my soul

Hunted, captured
Shipped, imprisoned, exiled
Enslaved, colonised, tortured
Indoctrinated, miseducated
Endured, persevered
Africa born within me
Emancipated
Shackles removed from my feet
Denigrated, segregated, separated
Cried at the top of my voice
Marched, picketed
Banished, boycotted
Wrestled, struggled
Assimilated, assassinated
Offering human sacrifices
Shackles removed from my hands
Freedom arrived in an a box marked with an X
Re-educated
Inspired, committed
Africa growing inside
Her human spirit flourishing
Love my people, love me!
One more hurdle to go
Remove shackles from my mind, our mind set
Capture my soul
Free my people
Liberate mankind from poverty of thought

My heart strings

Strumming a familiar melody
Resonating with my heart
My memories a song book
No chart toppers
Just evidence from another lifetime
An era that was
Music reminding me
The errors of my ways
Reminding me of that was
Humming a familiar tune
The same songs from before
A catalogue of greatest hits
Praying for harmony
Serenaded by rhythm
Pulling my heart strings
Soothed by the ambience of the cello
Violin strings tense
Pulling my heart strings
Drumming the sense into a being
Rattled by the electric guitar
Reminding me of a different time
When things were in concert
When I was a rock star
Now listening to the instruments
A soundtrack to a miracle
Pulling my heart strings
Writing my song
My heart pulling the strings
The world my instrument

Rumours of rain

Rumours of rain
A speculative phrase
Storms brewing
Violent pebbles eating away at the river bed
The scars deep
The anguish much deeper
The storm within a hurricane
Undercurrents eternal
Forever far away
Infinity the boundary of imagination
The last number
Rumours of rain
Thoughts planted by others growing in our minds
The storm within a hurricane
Awaiting an end of a natural disaster
The world in a blender
Disintegrate a nature of violence
An end of a storm
A sunny day away
When the world decides to show its true colours
A phrase becomes a promise
A weather report a phrase
Precipitation a kept promise
Drought a breach
Expectation dyed by the overcast surroundings
I love you a phrase
A promise to be a strong sail
The storm forever brewing
Undercurrents a permanent feature
Rumours of rain
A speculation of calamity
Skies always partly cloudy

Anticipating thunders showers of rain
Never planting the seed
Afraid to cross the river
Cultivating a breach of promise
Harvesting empty promises
A pebble in a storm on the horizon
Held captive by imagination

Epic

Breathing a reflex
Living a piece of cake
Topped with cream and nuts
Enjoying bubbles of oxygen hidden in chocolate
Inhaling and exhaling
The elements at your beck and call
Survival on the other hand
A matter of life and death
Living a leisure
Scrounging for oxygen not routine
Fighting to stay alive
Singing lullabies to the heart
Retouching memory
Anything to protract a demise
Dealt a blow
Playing the current hand
Love of living holding on
Body parts in survival mode
Making do an active exercise
Living passive like breathing
A by the way
A by-product of a struggle
Survival a must
Lifestyle an optional extra
Stuck in the basement of a triangle
Living merely a finishing touch
Survival an imaginative exercise like 3D cinematography
Living like extras on a set
Stars survive
Survival an epic

The Present

Emerging from the east
Each rising of the Sun
Bringing a possibility of punishment
Chinese water torture
Only without the water
Droplets of memory falling onto your lap
The constant splatter annoying
Looking at a semblance of a life
Particles of joy leaving you glistening with satisfaction
Surrounded by murky waters
Tortured by destiny
The circumstances an unwilling servant
Executing heavenly orders
Nearly killing a weaker man
The cause of the annoyance strengthening every sinew
Sharpening every thought
Strangled by the present
Freed by an exercise of thought
Liberty a mental state
A state of being
Coming to terms with the intricacies of existence
Beyond the constant splatter
On the other side of unchartered waters
Lies a pool of possibility
A free man
Baggage discarded
Tortured by the yearning for less of the same
Tired of more of the same
Life beckoning at this very moment
Laughter an achievement
Tears too much like droplets

Dampening the mood
Weigh down on possibility
Tortured by expectation
You'll never know how strong you are
Until being strong is no longer a choice

Nature's Revenge

Singing shosholoza
Muscles toned
The terrain flabbergasted
Astounded by the necessity for acupuncture
Pierced by pick-axe after pick-axe
Synchronised labour
Creating a domino effect
Pain passed from rock through sand to stone
Preparing a path to progress
Boulders excavated
Trees uprooted
Ecosystems ravaged
Singing in unison as they toil
The acappella melody soothing
Numbing the pain
The men united in purpose
Following the plotter's markings
The mountain diverted, averted, avoided
Sometimes tunnelled
Only the mountain keeps reappearing
Making the men toil harder
Their synchronised efforts not yielding
Seemingly in vain
Try as they may
To out manoeuvre the mountain
The mountain keeps reappearing
The men digging deeper
Their souls weary
Not paid to think
But beginning to ponder the point of their purpose
Despite their toil
Not arriving at progress

Beginning to question the wisdom of progress
Belted by the sun
Their shade uprooted
Their pick axes metamorphosised
No longer digging tools
Baying for the plotter's blood
The plotter cuts his losses
The men disgruntled
Victims of their shallow aspirations
Returning to their villages
Welcomed by a familiar sight
The mountain keeps reappearing
Their ploughing fields desolate
Livestock depleted
Families famished
The ecosystem to blame
A ravaged ecosystem bears the blame
Drought the diagnosis
The men ascend the mountain
Unable to pray for rain
The boulders of culture excavated
Unable to pray in their own language
Pain passed from generation to generation
The mountain laughs

My Lollipop

Draped in chocolate
A centre core of sweetness
Immersed in eye candy
Chocolate coated honeys
Clad in nothing but brown skin
Chocolate melting in the mouth
Telling the taste buds many stories
Amazed by the numerous textures
Shades of the same colour
A band of sweetness
Dark chocolate
Milky ways of oohs and aahs
Tantilising slabs of ecstasy
Melting the heart
Relishing chocolate cake
Biting into billions of bubbles
Black forest cake with cream
Every square inch soft like a chocolate muffin
Tasteful seduction
Candy was her name
Flattering the taste buds
Telling all sorts of stories
Tales of endearment
Sweet like a love story
Falling for flakes of fantasy
My tongue experiencing moments of luxury
Each nibble concentrated with different consequences
Sprinkled with fruit and nut
Spreading a smile
Licking her lips

Cotton Pickers

Please forgive me
I beg your pardon
Am about to step on your toes
Am kinda fed up
With you and your kind
Black folk in particular

No offence intended
But you getting on my nerves
Behaving like a scorned lover
Forever longing for acceptance

They ain't never gonna love you
Get with the program, get used to it
Nurturing hurt, perpetuating pain
Instead of harnessing anger
Generate a positive self-image

Sharpen your spear, your asseggai
Loving yourself is a start
If you don't embrace who you are
How the hell do you expect others to?

Just cos you been treated like dirt
Don't mean you're dirt
Stop being ignorant
Ditch the slave mentality

Embrace your African roots
Elevate yourself, educate yourself
You're the master of your destiny

Yet you give others power over you
Instead of being an African
Stand up and be counted
Amongst men and women who loved themselves
Loved themselves so dearly
Opting to die rather than remain a slave, remain silent

I beg your pardon
Am about to step on your toes again
Focusing on Slavery
Ignoring the Africans singing Negro Spirituals
The endurance to survive the cotton fields

Traumatizing your hair
Entertaining skin lighteners
Losing your essence
As beautiful as Ashanti gold is on Wesley Snipes' chest
No amount of gold can supplant your love for yourself
Your love of an Afro
Your nappy hair is a gift from God

Yet you persist to attempt to appease them
Fighting their wars, marrying them
Only to be paid with scorn and ridicule

Playing victim is disempowering
It defeats the purpose
Identifying with Slavery
Ignoring Africa
Harness your anger
Arm yourself with knowledge
Achieve something

You're not a descendent of slaves
Cotton pickers were Africans

The Matrix

Athletic as the body may be
Despite the obvious toned muscles
It is the soul
Lifting the combination of technique and co-ordination
Gliding it over hurdles
A combination of science and spirituality
Rumours from ancestors
The blood alone isn't enough
Something else paints the picture
My guess as good as yours
The essence of experience
An unheralded destination illuminating the picture
Sifting through a matrix
Twirling, leaping, somersaulting
While the body lies there
Laying in stately idleness
Visiting forthcoming attractions
Moments in time
Destinations desired by the heart
The soul transcends generations
Defying the laws of gravity
Going up when down is logical
No matter how illogical
The soul makes sense of things
Cultivating barren plains
Feeding a nation out of despair
Housing the body
The body merely a shovel
Pitiless without spirit
Yet, killing the spirit is a white lie
Killing the body a crime
Valuing the house
Ignoring the home

Puddles

Enthralled by her footsteps
Captivated by her words
Words spoken in honesty
Depicted by her poise
Her voice a mystery
Wanting to read her
Like Stevie Wonder would
Feel each pore on her skin
Write her a song
Play her like a piano
Decipher her
Bring her to an eruption
Capture the melody of her voice
Understand the meaning of her movement
Her hips saying so much
Not only confirming her gender
Highlighting who she truly is
The manner of her speech
Too deep for one life time
Her physique
Though accentuated by her blackness
Desiring her mind
Her body a bonus
Bringing meaning to words
Teaching them to prance to her movement
Dance to the rhythm of her hips
For she is deep
Making the oceans between
Seem like puddles in the road

Death Inevitable

Life everything between now and then
A dash between two dates
Death giving meaning to life
Placing parameters on wishful thinking
Death a fact of life
A comma in a short story
Sometimes a death is a birth
Some people live beyond the grave
Leaving an impression on this world
Death is inevitable
Some surrender to harsh realities
Destroyed by consequences of slavery
Dying before their time
People with a zest for life going against the norm
Challenging the surroundings
Dreaming big
Stretching the parameters
Negotiating with an inevitability
Daring to live
Remembering Africa
Living beyond the grave
Touching lives to this day
Living an act of denial
Squeezing a lifetime into a dash
Life a marathon of choices
Your outlook the most critical
Nobody wants to finish first in this race
A race against time
Some dying young and beautiful
A few campaigning for immortality
Establishing a legacy
Planting seeds and thoughts

Courting a dynasty
Only a mere mortal entertaining immortality
Seeking an understanding
Death not new to us
Giving life meaning
Death verifying a fact of life

Merry go round

A colourful wheel
Spinning in the playground
The giggles of toddlers filling the air
Laughing as one of them falls
Spilled by the wheel
Spinning out of control
The ride exhilarating
Mesmerising body parts
Juggling organs of thought
Sky diving made easy
The wheel spinning
The ride addictive
The stuff dreams are made of
Offered a single ride
Going where the wheel takes me
Holding on tightly
The possibility of falling part of the fun
The actual fall part of life
The tumble as exciting
Jumping back on courageous
Dusting off myself
Licking my grazes
Whilst others watch the wheel spinning
Always in the background
Afraid of falling
Too scared to live
Sometimes it spins out of control
Threatening my comfort
Adding to the excitement
Enjoying the ride
The spills part of the fun
Part of life in the foreground
Oh this merry go round

Perception

Between here and there
Lies perception
Everything a degree of sorts
Black from here to here
Indigo between this and that
An acceptable aspersion
A perception of sorts
Between wavelengths
Incidents of thought occur
Engaging in greatness
Sharing ideas with the like-minded
Entertaining espionage
Grappling to understand purpose
Life a pouch of secrets
A broadband with a vast bandwidth
Negotiating degree
Watching opposing poles
Interlocking alike mind sets
Breaking the ice with a warm smile
Nothing is concrete
We're all stuck in an emulsion
A metamorphosis of shape
Form merely an interpretation of physics
Expressing a variety of shades
All experiencing varying degrees of hardship
Liquid, steam, ice - expressions of water
People like molecules
Character a spectrum of personality
Greatness boundless, just is
Not from here to there
Precision a lie
The angle of sight so telling

My Back

It's been one of those days,
Those unexpected days,
When the world agrees with you,
Flatters you like they fatten sheep
Before the slaughter,

Always got to have your back
Even when the world buys you a cocktail
Especially when you're sailing the smooth seas
Stirring my drink with its umbrella
Cos it's only a matter of time
The rainy days may return at any moment
The rough seas
The dark clouds
Are forever lurking in the vicinity
Seagulls hovering like vultures in the Kalahari

Impatient for a misjudgement or two
Waiting to feast on your demise
Give in without a fight

I surrender my body
Yielding without a fight
Letting the elements do as they please
My soul soaring
The sails taut
Enjoying my cocktail so long
Watching the world dot my 'i's
Cross my 't's

'Cos when I got my back
It ain't me doing the watching
'Cos for starters
I can't see my back

Waiting for the elements to cross my path
So I can be humbled
Experience another lesson
Life's a never ending education
Holding onto the silver lining

Comfortable with destiny's promise
My location within the ecosystem
A reserved seat
Praying my ancestors intercede on my behalf
Book my place amongst peers
Asking the Almighty for tickets

With my back turned
Praying, you got my back
Indulging Judas
The guy who buys you a drink
Shares a toast with you
At peace with the state of affairs!
Ending my prayer with RSVP

Goodbye

You left in haste
You left without saying goodbye
Leaving your perfume behind
Impressions of your feet remain in the carpet
Visions of your long legs in my mind
Your scent is all over the house
Without an explanation
Without blowing me a kiss
Your earrings are still here
Am not surprised by the sudden departure
'Cos you know I loved you
Your words my music
Your presence my throne
Only if you weren't such a coward
Afraid of love
Too scared of consequences
Yet you do love
Too timid to express it
This is a first for me
Dumped for the wrong-right reasons
Normally I'm guilty as shit
Forget Valentine's Day
Stuff the roses
It's you I want
My only sin - was loving you to the bone
My mistake
Wanting to kiss the hurt away
Detach you from a past
Gently remove the thorns of pain
You must have felt the might of my love
Too afraid to love
Frightened of being loved
Too scared of the disappointment that may follow
Sometimes *'deja vous'* never arrives!

The season of reason is gone

No longer deliberating under the shade of tree
Detached from a common pain
Neglecting a sacred pact
A united front shattered
Broken by broken promises
Forgetting too soon
Freedom obtained with reason
I write what I like sparking a revolution
Creating a chain reaction, changing many a mind set
Identifying mental slavery as the arch enemy
Forgetting too soon
Freedom obtained with constructive engagement
Talks about talks
A *bosberaad* in the middle of nowhere
An *indaba* immersing itself into the vocabulary
Locals developing the language of negotiation
Gathering under a tree
Giving birth to a rainbow nation
Words have an untold power
Nkos' Sikelela i'Afrika for example
Giving a continent a mandate to stand up
Forgetting too soon, a gathering under a tree
The cornerstone of our civilisation
Heads of reason too afraid participate
Frightened by a general lack of understanding
Attention diverted by an illusion of comfort
The comfort of material a mirage
Shouting and chanting
Displaying a reasonable behaviour from another era
Forgetting reason is governed by parameters
Material conditions of everyday life – time, place, and motive

Forgetting too soon
The long walk to freedom a momentous journey
Now a marketing tool
The sole domain of the powers that be
Worshipping idols, colonisers inaugurating a messiah
Pinning our hopes on a false hope
Indigenous reasoning heckled
Native intelligence removed from the agenda
Dancing, shouting, singing
Entertaining the population instead of providing leadership
The populous singing along in a trance
Deferring a dream
Giving up on Great Zimbabwe
No longer deliberating under the shade of tree
Forgetting to think
Thought out of fashion
Pop culture offers no substance
The current state of affairs offering no substance
Forgetting too soon
No longer deliberating under the shade of tree
Engaging in gossip
Discussing personalities
Conduits of patronage
Small minds in abundance
Ideas and ideals out of fashion
Across the length and breadth of the continent
Shouting at the top of our voices
Demanding respect
Disrespecting the great leaders that we are
Ignoring the voice from within
Heckling the voice of reason

Forsaking courage
Forgetting too soon
The art of diplomacy a mere recollection
No longer deliberating under the shade of tree
Depicting my perspective
Writing in a foreign language
Highlighting the gravity of the situation
Black man wake up!
There is no messiah
Only a tree in a clearing in the veld
Words from a childhood echoing
Don't raise your voice, improve your argument
Discontent misplaced
The season of reason is gone

Quilt

Sometimes I wonder
Amazed by my largest organ
Being born black
Endowed generously
Blessed with the ability to withstand
Taking on the Sahara
Defeating the Atlantic trade
No amount of lashes
Misrepresentation
Nor miseducation
Diminishes its stature
A mirror image of rhythm
Making music despite the circumstances
A quilt of a common pain
Clothing the first citizens
Gift wrapping supermodels and the downtrodden alike
Stretching to beat microseconds
Giving gold a platform to shine
Basking in the glory
No sun screen necessary
Nourished with jet black arrogance
Tarnished by ignorance
Chocolate, cafe au lait, cream
A spectrum of coffee colour
The embodiment of what makes you black
Moistened with tears
Sometimes I wonder
Its tenacity to withstand amazes me
Sometimes it's good
To be the shade I am
Though averse to water sports
Dominating the gene pool

The whole point

Sparkling in maternal eyes
Spawning a population from love making
Communicated best with babble-speak
Love has a vocab of its own
Life teaching you to identify it
The way she looks at you
Her hungry eyes making contact with your insides
Wanting to devour you
Apprehension eating you from the inside
For without butterflies
It is not the real thingamajig
Love frighteningly beautiful
Our closest encounter with a burning bush
The apex of spirituality
Bonding two spirits with superglue
Making love to Neo-soul
Interrupted by vicious shagging
Two bodies going at it like gladiators
Fighting to the death
Collapsing in defeat together
Holding onto each other for no reason
Love expressed even better with body language
A hug a procedure with immense proportions
Allowing the heart a voice
Comforting insecurities
Establishing an ecosystem
Participants prone to doing strange things
All because of love
Dying and rejuvenating at will
Love has a life of its own

Drama Queen

When eventuality arrives
The body departs
Arriving where the spirit lies
The spirit is always on a reconnaissance mission
Pioneers aren't ground breakers
Merely followers of the spirit
Just like the body
Venturing to where the heart lies
Daring to cross battle-lines
Fight for freedom
The spirit is a boundless wandering soul
Seeking a secret garden
Enchanted by tranquillity
Not the quiet of a garden
The peace of derived surroundings
Eventuality is only a matchmaker
A reunion of body and soul
Eventuality is death for most
A dream come-true for a few
Sparking from desire
Everybody gets what they want
Eventuality gift wrapping the desired contents
The body a mode of transport
An identity book
The soul commands the elements
Pleads with the composer
Soul music a heavenly composition
Eventuality an instrument
Time a melody
A song with a message
Eventuality a drama queen

Etiquette

Everything a prescription
A medicine of sorts
Application guidelines compulsory
Tagged fragile
Packaged accordingly
Bound by etiquette
Manners make a man
The demeanour of a toast
Keeping within the norm
Forgetting my manners
Breaching a code of conduct
Conducting myself in accordingly
Lacking common courtesy
Depriving myself of a common decency
Handling myself shabbily
A discourtesy self-inflicted
Failing to peruse the conditions of sale
The terms and conditions
Despite the fine print
Whether external or internal
Everybody governed by a set of rules
An aura of sorts
The frequently asked questions not going away
Encrypted in the genes
Deep within bones
Lies etiquette
The user manual
The essence of a writer
A binding contract
A testament of a mind set

Urban Legend

(A tribute to Steve Biko)

Born into slavery
Forever free
Selfish with the soul
Generous of mind
Charitable with life
Medicine's loss
A nation's gain
Provoking radical thought
Irking my conscience
Your questions very personal
Your simplicity appreciated
Reflective of your nature
An embodiment of the modern African
An urban legend
An intellectual of the self
An everyday person
Ploughing neglected minds
Breeding blacks
Mobilising egotistical students into a force
Inspiring a generation
Wish you could see your harvest
Being visionary
Obviously you can
Your simplicity genetic
Inherited by your offspring
Wish it was contagious
So all can be infected
Simple yet profound
Your parents must have known
Christening you with responsibility
Embracing it with both hands and mind

I guess they had to kill you
You can't imprison thought
Your reasoning was high treason without the T
On a winter's day in '76 the struggle reached its turning point
Soweto grasped your reasoning, challenging the world
Bearing testimony to your influence
Walking on Bantu Biko Street a way of life
Black on Black validation
Making the pains worthwhile
I guess your mother would concur
Your generosity and charity
A product of the human face you identified
A face you identified with
Africa's human face
Underplayed by beneficiaries of your toil
Your sphere of influence is growing
Our grey matter blackening
I wish we could clone you
Mass produce you in the population
Mental liberation a destination
I write what I like my bible
My life the next chapter
One day you'll be famous
Like the other guy who died naked
'Cos you can't kill thought either
Your spirit, Frank Talk lives on
An urban legend to some
The truth

Falling

After midnight arrives
The next day begins
Awake like an owl
Watching regrets cascade
After midnight shows up
Dreams play themselves out
After midnight drive-in
Tumbling out of dreamland
Entering into a factory of dreams
Every day a drop in the ocean
Born in the dark of night
Falling into loving arms
Plunging into a pool of dreams
In a beautiful place
Like the gardens of Babylon
A terrace of beauty
After midnight arrives
Each day arrives at a different tier
Surrendering to its whims
Watching the sun falling into place
After midnight begins to arrive
Plunging into dreamland
Treading into ancestral lands
Succumbing to a deeper meaning
After midnight arrives
Dreams are planted
Each day a conveyor belt between tiers
Toppling kingdoms
Watching the midnight arrive
The last supper

An infinite longing

When a man cries
Expressing an infinite longing
To be a man amongst men
To love and be loved
Feel pain
Only then can others follow
To cry when hurt
'Cos that's what makes a man
For without tears he is incomplete
A strong man knows when to cry
The making of a man
An arduous responsibility
A difficult path at best
To be a man
A man must grow like an evergreen shrub
Banish the boy
Kill his dreams without severing his manhood
Deal with reality
Fearing what awaits a man
To be a man amongst men
Fall when the world demands
When should a man cry?
Only a man alone decides the appropriate moment
'Cos when a man cries
A damp admission of mortality emerges
The world in the waiting room
A man must fall from grace
Cry for goodness sake
End an infinite longing
Escape the myth
The strength of a man isn't infinite
But equal to the variety of ache he has endured
Only but a man
A king unto himself

Shackles

Shackles on our feet
Shackles in our hearts, minds and soul
Shackles from our recent past ringing in our memory
Suffocating our spirit

Too many black men behind bars
Confined to an empty existence
An inner city fence restraining our expression
Losing our essence, our dress sense
Our sense of self lost in desert of ignorance
Unable to dance to our rhythm

The chains of slavery dangling to this day
Tying us to evidence of a holocaust
Limiting our movement
Impeding our march
Our progress as a people placed on pause
Short steps placed on our giant strides
Our glorious history of achievement and innovation locked away

Shackles in our hearts
Driving a wedge between kings and queens
Destroying the extended family
Erasing a collective memory
Entertaining a genocide
Perpetuating a crime against humanity

Shackles in our minds
Bound to a lie
A negative perception of ourselves
Sibling rivalry sprouting like weeds in garden
Failing to follow our ancestors
To write what I like

Attached to a mentality
Despising one another by design
Disliking an innocent colour
A reflection of the Universe denied its place at the table
Losing our complexion, our make up
Drowning in a pool of bleach

Shackles on our feet
Shackles in our hearts, minds and soul
Shackles from our recent past ringing in our memory
Suffocating our spirit

Glorifying the ghetto
When the ghetto is no heaven
Following deities designed to demean us
Detouring our drive towards humanity
Despite the depiction
The description in scriptures
God is an African

Shackled to a degrading existence
Surely death is better
Rather we all die
Die a better man, woman, child
Lose these shackles
Die for an ideal
Decolonise the mind
Remember Africa
Resurrect our collective soul
Wake up and smell the coffee!

Anonymous Player

Addicted to an addiction
Body heat a narcotic
Drawn to softness
Suppleness a foreign phenomenon
Addicted to an ancient ritual
Drawn to the high
Stimulated by primal instincts
Genes wanting to swim
Adding finishing touches to a complete being
Hooked to the texture of compatibility
Biting into the bubbles of cake
Licking the cream of her face
The ritual of love
Addiction by nature
Natural selection a matchmaker
Missing the accompanying silliness
Holding hands
Laughing simultaneously
The journey to losing yourself
Ending in a cry of ecstasy
Becoming an item
Completing each other's sentences
Addicted to love
Infatuation infectious
Locking lips and hips
Addicted to the opposite sex
An anonymous player